Unveil Me

the complete duology
& other poems

Featuring the full collections of...

Unraveling Light & Darkness Undone

Elayna Mae Darcy

Magic Key Media

Unveil Me: the complete duology & other poems

ISBN: 9798375675183

Book Design by Elayna Mae Darcy.
Illustrations by Elayna Mae Darcy.
Front Cover Image by Elayna Mae Darcy.

Printing & Distribution by Kindle Direct Publishing.

First Edition, March 2023.

Magic Key Media
Philadelphia, PA 19134

For everyone who has ever
been afraid of making mistakes.
Consider this your permission to
make them, & to grow
beautifully from
them.

Unraveling Light

the complete collection

SELF

**I am unraveled.
A life illuminated.
Prepare to meet me...**

You

First,
I had to collapse
and admit to the power
I'd given my name,
and know that it had
become a black hole,
consuming who
I wanted to be.

I came undone,
a revelation that lasted
twenty-four revolutions
around the sun.

Across time and space
who I could be
called out to me,
a quiet voice,
somewhere beyond,
out in the void.

Alone, in the silence
with fabric sheets and concrete
separating me from the sky,
I heard her.

I found her.

And though she
spoke in a whisper,
I knew she spoke truth.

I am here.
I am light.
I am you...

Lantern

I illuminate the room.
By my light, your eyes can see.
Though I may burn out,
it will be to give you all of me.

Home

When first I was here,
I did not know
my own name
or how long it would
take to become it.
I did not notice
the glorious willow trees
standing tall behind me,
for all I could do
was stare blankly
ahead to a future
filled with maybes.

Back then I was still
a newly minted orphan,
already feeling spent
after all the things
life stole from me.
But before me,
I saw an infinity of possibility.

I was sure, even then,
in the kind of way
one can't describe with words,
but can feel in the notes of a song.
This would always be my home.[1]

And though this place is theirs now
so they might become and grow,
my heart will never leave here,
this I'll always know.

---

[1] This line was changed from the original publication to omit a reference to the H*rry P*tter books, given the author's transphobic rhetoric.

Named

That's not who you are,
they said, as if
I don't know myself.
As if my heart beats
in their body,
or my thoughts sound
in their mind.

It's hard to get used to,
they said, as if
hurting me for their
own convenience was fair.

Your name is X,
she said, not
giving a damn that I
only answer to Y.

I'm writing you up,
she said, as if
by being cruel, she could
somehow also be righteous.
But those with hearts
spoke sweeter words.

It's so you,
they said, as if
discovering that this
was the missing piece
to my spirit's puzzle.

It's beautiful,
they said, as if
they knew how much
and for how long
my soul had ached
to be called that word.

I'm so happy for you,
they said, as if
their words were
the hands of a healer.

This is me,
I'd say, as if
it was who I'd always been,
because in truth,
it was who I always was.

Punctuated

My body is an —,
some say it is unnecessary
or that it takes up too much space,
but it has a point to make,
and it won't let you go
until you've listened.

My mind is an !,
always running
high on energy,
feeding on excitement,
unrelenting and loud,
and ever without permission.

My heart is an *,
small, but important.
Blink and you'll miss it
but notice it and
you'll find clarity
and deeper meaning within.

My soul is an ... ,
Reminding you of more to come.
That the story continues
when this — body is done...

Starved

Some nights I wonder
if anyone will ever
see me...
really me...
not the me that
embodies the body
that magazines
would have me be.
A monster by Shelley,
one that must be
trimmed, cut,
and spliced into
a societal ideal
of beauty.

No one has ever
seen me...
the real me...

They see what
the world has told them,
convinced them,
is ugly.

The size of my heart
amounts to little
when the size of my body
consumes what you
think of me.

You call me fat,
or heavyset,
not realizing you've
made my soul
the heaviest thing about me.

You've put me
under pressure that says
that the weight of my body
means I deserve
the weight of loneliness
on my spirit.

You've rendered me
beyond what a diet can fix,
because I'm starved
of love you're convinced
I'll never be served.

Life Sentence

The depressive mind
has a problem with permanence
in which it convinces us
that every instance of pain
will be felt in perpetuity
for the rest of our days.
That one glance from a stranger
which lasted less than seconds is
a life sentence of
judgment and must mean
you are forever
ugly and unwanted.
The negative balance in your
bank account feels written into your skin,
forever inked so that
everyone sees and thinks
you will never amount to anything.

Atomic

There are days
when getting up
out of bed
is climbing Everest
and days when
forgetting that one thing
you had to do
is an atomic bomb
in your chest.

There are moments
when just being in a room
with other people
is like 10,000 arrows
drawn and ready
to fire at your face
for breathing wrong.

When the world
makes you hate
who you are,
existing becomes
a wide open ocean,
and you don't
know how to swim.

Existence

There's an ever
kindled fear that
this is it…
that I won't see tomorrow.

It's hard to shake
what's become fused
to my skin.

Will I still be
able to walk when
the shaking legs are
cut out from under me?

Will I still be
able to see when
my irises aren't
made of worry?

Will my voice still
sound when it has
screamed away
all its doubts?

Will I still exist when
I've stowed away
the worst of me?

Drowning

I can't stop fearing that
I'll never get better
and that soon will come
the final storm I can't weather.
I'll drown in it
with no way out,
the waves so loud,
no one hears my shouts,
as water fills my lungs,
just like my doubts.
I'll sink to the bottom,
buried beneath the sea,
because I could never
learn to believe that
I deserved to be.

Will

Typed it up and stared at it...
the little line blinking and
blinking and blinking,
a pulse
keeping with my own.

I want to press send,
but I think of who
my words might hurt
and I think of who
my actions might destroy
and I think of how different
the world will look
when I'm not in it...

Voices inside that
aren't mine whisper,
just do it,
hit send
press delete
on your life
post it,
tell them
the world
how much you
think they hate you...

Logic and reason
try to quiet the demons
that would have me believe
I'm worthless.

I must matter to
someone...
somewhere...
maybe...

I argue with the voices
trying to cast out their poison.

I AM LOVED.
I AM WANTED.
I AM JOY,
I scream at them.

you are alone.
you are abandoned.
you are despair,
they mumble back.

I erase the words
and type them again
and erase them again,
choking on air,
sobbing into my sweater,
as I read the words
one last time...

If I died tonight, would anyone care?

But my phone pings.
It's a snap from a friend.

When I reach to open it,
I see the brave kitten
on my home screen
as my hands are shaking.

But my friend wants to see me.
They want to see me tomorrow...

I glance to cards on a shelf,
sparkling with glitter,
and with love etched inside.

Beside them,
a pile of books.

Stories I haven't finished yet.

I'm sitting in a room,
with a roof over my head,
and a heater at my side
on a below frozen night.

I wipe the tears.
I erase the post.
I close the tab.
I reply to the message.
I feel something...

There's just an ember left in my heart,
but it's enough to spark a fire.

These times when loneliness
tries to take me, and when
the demon's whispers become thunder,
God whispers back, reminding me of my mission.

Go on. Fight. Love.

When I don't want to,
is when I must.
When I feel I can't live,
I will...

Sky

Noticed a break of blue
in the cloudy, darkened sky.
A reminder that
hope and colors
lie ahead, if I manage
to stay alive...

Gifts

Everything is a gift.

The reassuring ticking of a clock.
The quiet peace that ushers in winter.
The blanket tucked snug around my toes.
The starlight in their eyes when they smile.
The ink stains on my hands.
The hope I feel at dawn.

But life also gives us darker gifts.

The father who smelled like beer.
The blood in my eye from the rock thrown at my head.
The countless tears that stained my pages.
The bitter shiver of failure in my veins.
The mother who died in my arms.
The gnawing fear that I'll die
feeling the same way she felt.

...alone...

Every sadness,
and every kindness,
has been a gift.
Each one a tool—
palettes and easels,
brushes and paper,
charcoal and watercolors.
Every moment God gives me,
is another gift to help me
create myself.

Enough

No amount of you
will ever be enough,
the voices say.

I've come of age
in a cold hard time
that has lied to me
so much and so well
that I'd grown to believe
they were right.

You're not enough
because you weigh too much.
You're not enough
because you're broke too much.
You're not enough
because you love too much.
You're not enough
because you think too much.

No matter which way
they cut me or divided me
or tried to summarize me,
I was never enough.

But I've had enough.

So I'll become more
than they thought I could
because I've always been more
than I thought I was
because the secret is
I am enough.

LIFE

The wind is howling.
The internet is screaming.
What a noisy world...

First Memory

It was an earthen rainbow,
a sprawling sea of leaves,
bright reds, brilliant yellows, fading greens.

My family's packed in the van.
Mom's driving, always steering
our family forward,
though getting no more
credit than a stranger driving a cab.

I know these things now,
for losing her taught me much
that I wish I'd never had to learn.
But I treasure those changing trees.

I don't remember the
90s song played on the radio,
but I remember that earthen rainbow.
I remember the September breeze
on my tiny cheeks
in the same way I
remember my mother...
with love, and with peace.

First Morning

They made us wait
in the nice room
with the cozy chairs
and paintings on the walls,
as if the interior design
could calm away the chaos
of hearing the words
I'm so sorry,
we did everything we could,
she didn't make it...

Waiting for my sister
to arrive at the hospital
broke me only further.
I had always tried
to keep it together for her.
But this time I couldn't.
There was nothing
left of me to hold on to.

When we got home
from the hospital,
the rain was at last slowing down
and the sky became the
kind of golden rose that it does
after a fleeting yet powerful storm.

As I looked up to the heavens,
tears returned, and I raged that my mother
no longer stood on the Earth.
But I was grateful at least
that she had been welcomed home
to such a glorious, resplendent sky.

Your Name

I wish I could have
known you before
a bottle became
your beating heart and
your veins became malt liquor.

I didn't know
until my twenties that
we shared a favorite song,
but by then it had been
ten years since you'd been gone.

I wonder often if you
could have been my friend.
If your heart hadn't
become a bottle,
maybe you wouldn't
have met an early end.

There's the dad I keep in my dreams,
who gave me books, cards with Snoopy,
and who sang me to sleep.
The memories with that dad are few,
but they're my most beloved just the same.

If only your blood hadn't
run cold like a beer,
maybe then,
I could have
kept your name.

They Were Stars

My parents were always stars.
I looked up to them when I was small.
They glimmered bright,
giving me hope.
It was not until I grew up
that I learned they were
never as simple as
I believed them to be.

They were complex, flawed,
burning out, and farther away
than I could have ever imagined.

But even though
they have both long since faded
in their own unique supernovas,
when I look closely
in the darkness,
what light is left of them
still shines to meet my eyes.

Nostalgia

The word evokes in most
Nickelodeon or N*Sync
or any of the other trappings
of our childhoods.
But for me, nostalgia has always
emerged in ways that
to the world might seem strange.

Backstage darkness,
the smell of lumber,
the hum of light fixtures.
12 scoop ice cream sundaes
from Friendly's after
every special occasion,
and lying in the freshly
mown grass of the football field.
Candle wax between my
fingers while lying on the driveway.
Nights looking for meteors,
and cool, rainy mornings
in the shadows of stone history
when we were hoping for a sunrise.

Nostalgia tastes like
Charlie's greasiest pizza,
smells like sweet incense,
feels like warm pavement,
and looks like starry skies.

Size of Stars

I sit in the shadows
of these lording over towers
which reach up and up and up,
trying to shake the hand
of the heavens.

At night they become
citadels of steel,
with fireflies for windows,
illuminating the night
even as they blot out
the galaxies above.

Sometimes I wonder,
what are these towers
to the size of stars
or to the solar system?

What are these tiny
skyscraper toys to
the One who made everything?

What are fourteen stories of metal
to fourteen billion years
of stories that fill up the cosmos?

It is nothing shy of a miracle to
imagine that God cares
for these tiny skyscrapers
and the lives within them
as much as They care for me,
and for you,
and for all of the heavens.

Magic Hour

Magic hour truly
is a name for a time
unlike any other.
What else but magic
could explain the way
the sun falls into
the bed of the horizon?
What else but magic
could describe the wonder
that I feel watching
silhouetted trees become
rogue brushstrokes against
a painted, glowing sky?
What else but magic
could express the promise
of adventure that lingers
in the air once stars
blanket the world?

Beacons

Stormy skies.
Ideas about to pour.
Rattling metal cars
on rain-slicked rails.
But then,
OPEN YOUR EYES
AND I SEE THE SUNRISE.

Day's breaking as the night's falling.
Broken rooftops are racing by,
with fear bounding from
one to the next like a superhero,
chasing a masked villain they
cannot name, only to realize,
that the villain is all around them
and inside the walls.
The real villain is
the system hiding in the corner
behind broken glass
and used box springs
and the lie that
you made this mess yourselves.

The rain made everything greener,
but the sky's still getting grayer,
making murals into beacons,
the only reminders that life
and love and color
still exist.

Empty Chair

The light is warm,
the feeling is comfort,
the aroma is robust espresso,
and the chatter is in
equilibrium with the soft indie music.

They all seem to be
functioning and focused and free...
though because I'm human,
I'm aware that's not true.

It's strange to explain
that I know we're all in pain
while all the while feeling
singular in my sadness,
and the thoughts banging
at my mind's door.

The souls you share space with
wouldn't notice if you weren't here.
The glint of amber sunlight
caught in your eye
would fall upon an empty chair
as if you were never there.

Even as the clownfish patterned pills
ease my mind, they don't erase
the latent pain or make
the sadness remain at bay.
But they keep me functioning, focused, and free
enough that I can try to be
just another face in the warm cafe light.

Every Corner

Trading in SEPTA for the Sound
as a new adventure begins.
As I ride these new rails
through fog, my mind
becomes clear.

I'm meant to be here.

In this moment,
three thousand miles from home,
I'm by myself, but never alone,
because to every corner
of this world that I go,
God is with me,
inside of me,
and around me.
From Cecil B., to Othello, to Waverly,
the Spirit of all
that was, is, and will be,
is part of me.

Signs

The sun sinks over my city.
Whiskey on my breath
lets me see her beauty
that's often hidden from me.
More sun stains my pages
as I write these words,
casting shadows of rings,
and fingers, and pens on
my journal's 6x9 paper world.

Through the window
there's a story made of signs,
and I can't help but wonder
what it has to say.

HERE YOU CAN.
ONE WAY.
ANY TIME.
ALL THE WAY.
STOP.

Brick after brick after brick.

EXCEPT PERMIT.
FOR SALE.
BEWARE.
DO NOT ENTER
THE GOSPEL.
ALL AMERICAN.
CLOSED.
A beautiful mural.

TRUE WORLD.
NORTH PHILADELPHIA.
THIS IS YOUR CITY.
NO STOPPING.

RESPECT.
WE MUST BE THE CHANGE.
EMERGENCY.
MAZES.
PAGES.
DIAMONDS.
Home.

Notifications

The phone blinks and my heart jumps.
Another thumbs up for my existence.

The phone blinks and my spirit sinks.
Another troll drops in to say I'm #TheWorst.

The phone blinks and my mind thinks.
Another article that leaves me hopeless.

The phone blinks and my head shakes.
Another notification that I can't escape...

Shadows

Figures pass me by.
Beyond the window they stroll.
Never touching me.

2018

We didn't need Netflix
to end up in the Upside Down.
We built it ourselves
when we let truth
be burned to the ground...

Red, White, and Blood

The saddest truth is
that we were never better,
and your "greatness"
was a myth and a lie.
Fed to the knowledge-hungry
minds of our children
so often and so young,
that before we even knew it,
we were addicts to the lie
of a free country.

We believed it was one
built on promise, togetherness,
and equality.

You branded it
onto our brains when
you forced us to stand
and pledge allegiance
to a flag made of blood.

Red blood,
for the lives lost.
The people you slaughtered
to build your picket fences.

Blue blood
is woven as the background to the stars,
because you believed your money
mattered more than lives.

White blood,
for your bigots who died
to "protect" a culture
that believed that those

who were black brown or anything other
deserved to be ripped from their mothers
to serve you.

As a child, I pledged to
your red, white, and blue blood,
not knowing the truth.
I thought the star spangled
colors stood for something good.

I wish I had known it was lies.

But when I look to the truth
with eyes wide open, I see...
This place was never free.

So I stand with the people
who don't look like me.
I try every day, to shut up
and listen to their truth,
their history— the honesty
classrooms kept from me.

I cannot change what's been done,
but I can help change what's to come,
with a mind that's open,
and with a heart beating as one.

Believe

There's times when
the way of the world
hurts so much that
I ask myself,
how did we get here?
How did we let hate
infect us when
our natural state is love?
Why are there so,
so many humans who believe
that fire and fury will make us great?

Vitriol bites with deadly venom
at the good and the light in the world.

Online,
in the streets,
in our hearts...
the poison seems to have won.

Yet the only reason that the demons
are so among us is because
we invited them in.
But they don't have to win.

A tweet, with love.
A smile on the street.
A hard conversation with a friend.
A willingness not to give up
even when all appears lost.
Hope can be eternal.
Love can be impenetrable.
Faith can be unstoppable.
But only when we believe together.

Still Beating

When I look at all
the wrong happening
in the world,
I can feel my heart breaking.

But if I have a heart
that is breaking,
it means I have a heart
still beating,
and some days,
that is hope enough
to keep fighting.

LOVE

Magic in their smile.
Constellations in their eyes.
My heart's still. Waiting...

One

As a little girl
I dreamed in rainbows,
stars streaming through my hair,
chasing the promises on the horizon.

Fairy tales told me
one day my prince would come
and despite the princesses
that sometimes captured my heart,
I buried that piece of me
so well that even I
didn't believe it was real.

But then life got
RENT apart by a single word,
one that broke my world
like a sparkling geode cracked open...
bisexual.

A prince could come.
So too could a princess.
I was no longer a mermaid
without a voice.
I was no longer a sleeping princess
without a choice.

I was me.

Free to save myself.
Free to love myself,
to love anyone who
might become the one.

We're Here

I thought coming out
would be triumph and kisses,
but too much of it has been
painful and dismissive.

Not gay enough to be gay,
not straight enough to be straight,
You're greedy.
Confused.
Indecisive.
You're fake.
I've become one of
the letters the initialism forgets.
To be bi, trans, or ace
means you're shown less respect.
Intersex, demi, pan, and queer,
we're tired of reminding
the rest of you we're here.
And so we fight for each other,
until equality is real,
and maybe then,
I pray then,
that our hearts might heal.

Stolen

I asked you online before we met...
please don't...
Apparently you only heard
the first eight letters of my words.

I thought, maybe I wasn't clear?
Maybe he didn't hear?
I took on the blame,
and despite my fears,
I gave him the second chance
that all the "nice guys"
claim they are so deprived of.

But this time, I was firm.
Do not kiss me again
until I tell you I am ready...

He apologized, agreed,
and said he would respect me.

I wish he had left my mouth
as empty as he did his promises.

This time, unwelcome arms
wrapped around me, hands groping.
His lying tongue was down my throat,
leaving me choking on his words
that meant nothing, because my comfort
took the back seat to his desires.

He caught his bus,
leaving me on the sidewalk,
defeated, and full of a fire
that I wished I would never have to feel.

He never touched me again
because I never gave him
chance number three
to make a prop out of me.

But sometimes still,
I feel the smoldering rage
of the fire he started inside of me that night.

My first kisses should have been
decisions I got to make.
But ever since, I've fought to make sure
the rest are no one else's to take.

Loved

It is hard to know
if I have ever been in love
when I have never been loved.

My remaining family does,
and so do my friends,
but when it comes to romance
it feels my heart may never mend.

I'm longing to know
if anyone will ever care,
but my hand keeps reaching out
catching nothing but air.

The Lesson

I wonder what
we could have been
if you hadn't decided for me
that I was too good for you?
Maybe we could have been
if you had just believed
you could be cared about.

Though our time has passed,
I've never stopped hoping
that you found your happiness.
For even now,
I believe exactly what
I believed then...
you have always been
worthy of being loved.
I hope it is a lesson you have learned.

Read Me

Sometimes I think in red ink,
constantly correcting my thoughts,
and crossing out the wrong pieces of me,
some days spent hating the lines
so much that I wish I could
rip out the pages of me.

I'm a first draft that
no one wanted to read,
a recklessly thrown together
work of prose left abandoned
in a bargain bin.

But when you look at me...
I become poetry.
I imagine if ever you kissed me,
we would become
a sweeping fantasy.
Your smile is my favorite story.

Yet the greatest tragedy
is that you've never read me.
What an epic we could be
if only I had the
heroine's courage to ask...
could you ever love me?

Our Star

I watched you
loving her wishing ever
that I was her.

You created with me,
told stories with me,
and read into
the deepest parts of me,
never knowing that
I'd give everything
just to be seen by you
the way you look at me
in my dreams.

We captured moments,
we crossed universes,
we invented beings
and all the while,
with you never knowing
what you've always meant to me.

Maybe by writing it down
and setting it free,
I'll finally be able
to say aloud the unspoken truth.

Maybe you'll read this
and just know, or maybe all this
will fade at the end of this page.

But while I can't imagine
if you and me will ever
become an us,
no matter what,
there are remnants of my heart
that will always be yours.

In the corner of the cosmos
we created together,
a star will ever
shine for you.

Hiraeth

Looking at your smile
conjures in me a hiraeth
that has nothing to do
with ground once stood upon
but everything to do
with missing the heavens
I am certain we were
sent to one another from…

Rebels

To ask to hold your hand
would be an act of rebellion.
To kiss you
would start a revolution.
Maybe loving you
could save the world...

Waiting for You

There's a perfect night
that we all wait for,
the kind that could only
be crafted in dreams.
In mine, there's no
dramatic carriage rides,
candlelit dinners,
or diamonds of any kind.
Whoever you may be,
it would be just you and me,
spending a summer night
on Rocky's steps while
it gets so late it becomes too early,
and together we watch
the sunrise over Philly.

We hold each other's hands
spending the whole night
laughing and talking and thinking
about the universe.
I never dreamed for
that mysterious one-night lover
that I would never see again.
I've dreamed of someone
so genuine and silly
who isn't afraid to be
hopelessly in love with their best friend.

I don't know if we've ever met,
or if you're still waiting out there for me.
But I have always known that somehow,
someway, this night I've dreamed for us
will come to be.

Harmony

I worry that life won't
write me a love story,
and that my adventure
will be all on my own.

But then I remember
those who are with me,
loving friends, treasured family.
I'm never truly alone.

The stories made me believe
that I cannot live without them,
that my options are restricted
to a partner or to sadness.
It's taken far too long
for me to understand that that's madness.

I still dream of a love
that can last beyond eternity.
But until then I am here,
and until someone else
loves me, I'll sing
my own harmony.

Someday

I tell myself it won't
always be like this
and that one day
someone will bind to me
like I'm their harbor
and my heart's where
they've cast down their anchor.

I've tried to imagine
who they will be,
but when your heart
can love his heart
or her heart
or their heart,
the beautiful possibilities
spin round in infinity.

Will she be a wonderer?
Will he be a dreamer?
Will they be a stargazer?
Will we become each other's?

Faith and belief that
the Lord knows my loneliness
gives me hope that
the space beside me
won't be ever empty.

But until I feel
their hand in mine
and until I hear
their name, it's time
for me to embrace my lonely
and learn to love myself.

CREATE

Words are in my blood.
My bones are built from stories.
Dreams ignite my soul.

Torch

I am leading the way,
journeying through generations.
I turn the darkness into day
so you might bring alive creations.

Say Me

Gotta get these words out,
they've fermented long enough.
These vines of ideas
getting intertwined
in my mind until
a narrative pours.
Emotions demanding,
Feel me.
A story begging,
Tell me.
Words pleading,
Say me.

Correction

They said,
Your head is up in the clouds!

I kindly corrected them.
No, but my spirit is up in the stars...

Creation

There's nothing like
the pressure to create.
The way that a story
builds and blooms
in the mind feels like
a miracle every time.

Synapses are firing off
and then suddenly,
a hand is moving,
and ink is flowing,
until a soul is spilling over,
rushing and insistent
as a river set free.

Thought stained pages
carry the story.
Some days are beautiful,
bathed in glory.

Yet some still drip
with a depression so dark
and so deep and so dense
that it pulls me in.

Those hours, I become a star
collapsing inward, still breathing,
but scarred.

Though always,
onward.

Pain washes away
when joy surges forth,
and we are baptized in
the promise of tomorrow.

To create is to never stop.
It is to breathe
and to know
every moment
we grow,
and something new
begins.

Poetry

Poetry is a form
of emotional osmosis.
It is absorbing the way
everything from the
breaking up of two people
to the
breaking down of North Philly buildings
makes you feel.
It is taking in particles
of meaning through your skin
until words begin
bleeding from the ink
between your fingers.

The Dream

In my dream,
I knew the smell of time,
as I watched the birds
find home.

You kissed me
again and again,
as we ran the ruined halls
searching for something
we couldn't name,
finding nothing but
empty rooms and broken desks
and each other...

The tree tops
burned crimson as I sensed
the smell of time.
Then you kissed my neck
while all the birds found home.

Bloom

The warm sun
on my back tries
to make doubt bloom
from my spine,
but with the words
and the meanings
and the questions
bound up in pretty papers
before me, I'm trying
to plant hope.

I have dreams blossoming
in my brain which
demons made of weeds
seek to choke out and kill.
But my still, small voice
reminds me to give
fear no quarter here.
When doubt screams,
love must shriek
and hope must hold
the fear like a friend
it once knew
who has changed.

The hope knows
that fear and doubt
were once flowers too,
but ones with poisoned soil.

So love and hope,
though small and quiet,
nurture and forgive
the fear and the doubt
until they remember their colors,
they remember their names...
they were once joy and faith...

Through love and hope,
they bloom once more,
and with the help of
the sun on my back,
the garden along my spine
blooms and grows and sings.

Power

Universes in my fingers
bring words and worlds alive.
Star clusters in my brain
bring people and places together.
Infinity in my heart
gives life and love a voice.

God has given me
a sliver of Their legacy—
the ability to create.
They have given me
a nose to smell memories,
a mouth to whisper musings,
eyes to witness moments,
ears to experience music,
hands to excitedly make.
They have given me
all that I need for
a life lived magically.

Love and light,
imagination and dreams,
are more than sentiments,
they are our weapons.

I wield them knowing that
each moment that I fight,
and each moment that I create,
I am waging war on hate
with the sources of true power.

Rising Tide

Don't keep me from dreaming,
plays the music in my ears,
as a mosaic of inspiration
settles and dries.
The people I've seen
and the dreams I've had
become one, because
like the Spirits said,
a rising tide raises all ships.

With their words
and their hearts,
new ideas flourish into being.
In this sea of creative minds,
I do not swim alone.
I am side by side,
swimming on together,
in a rising tide
that lifts us all.
You and me,
them, her, and him,
we and us.
We swim together
until we break the surface
and bask in the sunlight
of our dreams.

Inward

With headphones on my ears,
the people around me become mimes,
moving their eyes and
mouths and hands,
saying things I can't understand
because I'm trying
to listen inward.

What does my heart tell me?

This I have always known...
I am meant to imagine and to make
and here among all this silent chatter,
I can hear inside.
Between the music
and between the lines,
hide words and hope
that only I am meant
to bring alive.

I'll Be

I can only be
who I am for when
I try to be other,
it's a lie leaving me smothered
and crushed beneath
the weight of expectations.
When a pen is in my hand,
I feel my power surging,
my spirit growing into
the flower of the seed
it always was.
I don't rhyme all the time,
nor will I adhere to
the standards which steer
the ships of society's consciousness.
I'll be who the fuck
I wanna be because
all I can be is who
my maker made me.

Screw proper verse.
Damn the shoulds.
Destroy the demands
and fuck all the plans
that people think
they get to have for me.
I'll be the magic
that I imagine,
I'll be the dreams
that I fathom,
I'll be the strange
I hope to see in the world,
because I'm the only me in the universe...

Boundless

I will never forget
the moment I became boundless.
There was a settling in my soul,
a confirmation of truth
in an instant...
I can create anything.

I'm home with
a pen to command.
I'm alive with
a camera in hand.
I'm breathing when
painting things,
I'm believing when
my voice sings.

I am an artist
who did not think
outside the box,
but rather drew it
into something new.
I filled it with
words and with colors
and with all the others
I've ever made.

I didn't let them
tell me what kind
of artist I could be.
I became the artist
I am.
Just me...

inspire

i cannot know if these words will make sense but inspiration never really does it is this strange and ancient nagging in the deepest places of my being that begs me to be freed inspiration is leaping breaths and passionate fury leaving me teeming with magic bursting with wonder and longing to speak it is every time new and different and yet full of familiarity like a friend i have just met but feel as though i have always known it is butterflies beneath my feet lifting me towards the sun it is the smell that makes me time travel to places i had forgotten it is the way the wind on my cheeks when i close my eyes feels like whispered kisses from the cosmos inspiration has no form nor frame but is a picasso of abstract joy and chaotic pain that compels my spirit to create it is all at once a supernova of the soul an elegant ember of an idea and a cosmic complexity that has been waiting for me since cells formed and consciousness was born more rewarding than any achievements more fulfilling than any days labors more satisfying than sex inspiration feels more real than my body it feels more real than my fingers it is the same energy that i was forged from i am an idea made alive i am a spirit who will survive these words may not make sense but they are all i have to convey what inspiration has meant to me this child of the heavens who somehow continues to be...

Spirit

Inside the skin of one,
I possess a spirit of many.
While I stand alone,
I'm made up of
millions of instances
of existences
of experiences
and of atoms.

I walk around with a body
that's lived on one lonely world.
But inside I fly free
with a spirit that's kissed
the edges of forever.

We are none of us one.
We are all of us many.
Plural singularities
made of matter
and memories.

CHANGE

We break and we bend,
but we never stop being.
We are forever...

Audacity

Aspire to have
the audacity of the bud
that dares to bloom in winter.

Born

Be who you were
before you were born
and you will become
who you were always meant to be...

I Am

The sun comes out
but the ground remains
icy and cold and solid,
and it reminds me
too much of who
I can sometimes be...
a warm sun smiling,
giving what light I have
to the ones I love,
while inside and on the ground,
I'm broken, hardened,
and freezing to death.

It took an inviting,
an embracing of something
that made me bigger on the inside,
to understand that the sunny sky
could melt the cold below.

Because always and ever
I am both.
I am a world.

I am sunlight and snowfall.
Muggy evenings and bright mornings.
It is that always and ever
being everything all at once
that reminds me
I was never meant to be singular.
I am darkness.
I am light.
I am...

Highs and Lows

Time ticks, unrelenting clicks,
a reminder of forward motion,
an insistent ocean with
a tide that abides by the moon.

I wish I could be as consistent.

For though I be persistent,
I can't keep my life
in time with a single rhythm,
a balanced ebb and flow is something
I have never known.

The world is ending, or all is well,
I'm basking in heaven, or drowning in hell.
Mastering balance ever evades me.
I'm a result of the highs and lows that made me.

I want to breathe even, to know calm and stillness,
but a mind ever on a precipice
is a penetrating illness.
So I breathe and use my pen,
to try and ease my mind,
so I do not succumb to
the highs and lows of time.

Keys

My symbols of hope
left waiting for me
when I needed them most.

On the ground along
paths I hadn't walked before,
placed into my hand
when I needed to feel sure,
turning what I thought
were solid walls
into doors.

On the day I moved in,
and once when I moved on,
on the set of my thesis,
and my twenty-seventh year's dawn.
When I questioned my story,
when I was about to be hired,
they've become cosmic reminders
forged in heaven's fires.

Each key has a message
that I am never alone,
unlocking a way forward
to adventures unknown...

Beauty

The Post-it on the mirror
spoke when I felt alone.
You Are Art,
the small paper said,
surrounded in hearts,
giving me reasons
to start to believe,
that this season of doubts
too shall pass.
It won't be long
until I'll be free,
joyful, and am finally
able to see my own beauty.

Sunsets

Signals and sunsets and signs,
things that make us read
between the lines of our lives
to rationalize moments...
that which makes us alive.

To bear witness
to such things
is to know God,
to see creation,
and experience the sensation
of the souls we've been given
and know that the
universe is in our veins.

The power isn't just higher.
It's inside.
Always growing,
waiting with patience
for us to notice.

A priest's hands
or knees on a pew
are not what we need
to open our minds
or to know that love is stronger
and that hope lasts longer.

So until my final breath,
I'll keep a weather eye
on the horizon line for the
signals, and sunsets, and signs to remind,
we mustn't ever give in.
We must love, continue, and awaken.

North Star

I am heaven's compass,
a guide from the dawn of time.
And though my light be ancient,
it has made wanderers into the wise.

Uncertainty

Not long ago,
I befriended uncertainty,
taking what had once
been my enemy and instead,
choosing to love it dearly.
We talk often now,
late into the umber hours.
I ask questions to which
I have long wondered
what the answers might be.
Yet I am met every time
with a knowing smile
and an encouraging
whisper of,
wait and see...

Becoming

Twilight and dawn,
are my beloved times
for the same reason
my heart belongs
to fall and spring.
Neither is complete,
they exist in flux,
always in between
in the process of becoming
something they weren't before,
but now will be until
a new day breaks.
I like to think
my spirit is a season
like fall or spring
and my heart is a time
like twilight or dawn.
For every fallen seed,
a new something grows,
and for every night
that the sun sinks into the sky,
in the morning, it always
and ever returns to rise.

We Are

I don't know if I am any good at this but I know it is something I must do. If my brain isn't painting words or creating worlds it feels alone, haunted, and unheard. I dream to be seen as more than what I've been because when the world has attempted to interpret me they have always been wrong because all along they have eaten society's lies that to be a certain size means as a thinking, feeling being, you must be compromised.

This, I can no longer abide.

And so I keep writing with the hope that it will make society see I am inviting them into my heart to understand me and to view me more complexly as a being, who though maybe broke, is richly living life. I will not be bound by expectation, I will breathe in liberation knowing I am made as I am because my Maker has a plan for me to share my stories, and help others see their glory for we are all of us made of the same substance as the stars and the dust of the galaxies far, beyond what we've ever been allowed to believe that we are. We are warriors. We are wonders. We are scarred. But still, we are...

Coordinates

An address only goes so far
in explaining where
and when we are,
for our coordinates
in the cosmos
matter more than
corner streets or
country crossroads
in the eyes of
the Artist that painted us here.

Storm

Through thunderstorms
And floods of self doubt,
I pull on my holey shoes
and keep going.

I don't know how,
but I imagine it is
thanks to my words
and my faith
that keeps flowing.

There's a current inside me
which I can't control,
an upstream rush
of stories and hope.

When I feel like I'm drowning
I'll remember to swim,
because I'm the
heart of a storm,
about to begin...

Brave

You, brave child,
are the reason for my words.
The universe conspired to bless us both,
for in meeting and sharing our pain,
we can begin to recover.
Our shared hope, a healing rain.
They called me brave
for speaking my truth,
but the fact remains that
these words were
always for you.

* * *

Darkness Undone

the complete collection

OTHERS

We walked through shadow.
Your hand in mine, guiding me
to a place called hope.

With Love, Your Story

Dear Storyteller,

Pen me a promise
with your ink-stained fingers.
Promise me you won't
let my words
go unsaid.

Pledge to me with your
loneliness-stained lips
that you won't
forget about me,
that you'll
tell me to the world
even if their
lie-stained ears
refuse to listen.

Vow to me
you won't let me go
until my adventures
whisk away the
hope-stained hearts
of the readers who
most need to
believe in something
bigger than any of us.

Swear to me
you won't give up on me—
and most importantly—
yourself.

With Love,
Your Story

Give The Universe

You have always been
          a bud, fit to bloom
who fought so hard
          through rock & soil
to be here
          with your soft beauty
and handsome bravery
          and inspired brilliance.

Your eyes always fixed
          on outer space, gazing
at other worldly suns.
          But when I look at you,
I see stardust sprung
          up from the ground,
a constellation of
          petals and thorns
to whom I wish
          I could give the
                    universe.

The Strangers

They sit huddled
by the fence
speaking words
I cannot hear,
but I like to
imagine they are
marveling at
life's mysteries
with me.

The Poet

Under the moon
& unseen stars
& the evening
Germantown air outside
Uncle Bobbie's bookshop,
I soaked in
the magic and
the hope of
the poet I look
up to the most.

She told me
to tell my story
before anyone
could take it.
She spoke of
choices and dreams
and how to fight
until I'd made it.
She asked the
young people
for their questions
and their art,
and for me,
she lit a fire and
reignited my spark.

The Librarian

No words
could ever fully convey
what a safe haven
you made for me.

In that musty
little library,
you showed me
that *myself* was enough,
that books could be
portals to other worlds
and places for me
to find peace.

With those scribbled
passes to get me out
of homeroom,
you showed me that
strangers could be
kinder than family
and that words
were the most
powerful form of magic.

So much of who I am
was molded in those mornings,
talking with you as
we put away books
and mused about life
in ways that made me
feel more seen than
I'd ever been.

I'll forever carry
that joy you gave me
simply by listening
to my stories and
assuring me they
were worth chasing.

Divine Secrets of the Driveway Sisterhood

We share a tapestry
of memories
woven from midnight summers,
candle wax & pavement,
the smell of
burned paper edges
covered with inscriptions
of deepest wishes.

Feathers and the
dust of crushed geodes
and a broken glass
symbol of the trinity.

That is what you were to me.

A somehow holy
set of sisters, together
in solidarity through
all those high school
trials & uncertainties.

Life led us through fights
where we faced demons, and
I know not everything
that we were then
remains now.
But I've never forgotten
laying on blankets
while we imagined how
life would look
when we grew up.

One of you
once said,
"I say this with
stars in my eyes..."

and I've long regretted
that I don't remember
the rest of your sentence.

But those eight words
captured the essence of
our driveway summer magic,
where we were more infinite
than anything else
in the world.

Those football field
sunrises by the
middle school
are nestled in my bones,
reminders that when life
gets boring, there is always
something beautiful
in the simple.

That three kids
who started out
strangers
could become sisters
across space
and through time.
That love never breaks,
and teenage hope
never dies.

Soulmates

I used to believe
that soulmates
were singular.
A one-to-one
relationship in everyone's
life, no room
for others—
no chance at
mistakes.

But the more
years I spend here
on this rotating rock,
the more I realize
that our fates
have many faces.

A soulmate
can be a lover,
a mother,
or a friend.

They are the humans
who you find
home in.

Collective Strength

We are so much more
than any employer
said we were.
Our worth never
determined in
the clocked hours
we worked, or how
professionally we
did (or didn't) dress.

In this time of
start-ups & trust funds
we forget that we
are ancient & magnificent
with every element
of Mother Earth
inside of us.

Fire—our passion burning.
Water—our hope like a tide, surging.
Air—our lungs quietly breathing.
Earth—grounding us in meaning.
Ether—free souls, ever being.

We have always been
wonder & worthy
without needing to
ask permission.

Our hearts hold more
value than any salary.
The love within us
more expansive
than galaxies.

A Place Where You Find People

An entire generation
laid out before me
in their revelry,
and I, the fly
on the wall.
The latest seed
to be planted in
the soil of this
community
that has been tended
with hardworking hands
and watered with love.
Husbands & coworkers,
wives & friends,
partners & persons...
so many lives
changed along the way,
all because of
an idea that this
"is a thing we
do together...
a place where
you find people..."

Watch You Go

Here at the
end of all things,
I'm still just
wishing you would
believe in yourself.
Because somehow
in all the things
you were selfish about,
it was never
love or patience
or kindness
for yourself.
I pray that
one day, you
understand
we never wanted
to watch you go,
but we could not
continue to
watch you
eat yourself alive.

The Wrong Family

I wish our blood
meant more,
but I guess it
never did.

The friends I've had
have held my hand
even as you
left me reaching
for empty air.

They helped me
sail safely through
every tempest
life tossed at me,
while you sat
somewhere on a shore,
peacefully pretending
that I was lost
at sea.

Yet still
I long for a day when
I share DNA with
a family who cares,
who understands
and celebrates
just how much love
I have to give.

What You Left Me

In my feelings
but out of body...
soul drifting somewhere
abstract between
then & now,
somewhere still
somehow filled
with all the
hope you left me.

That was my true
inheritance from you,
the kind no
insurance policy
could give or promise.

You left me with
kindness & grit,
with a spirit that
while generous,
never took shit
from anyone.
Fierce love
from a heavy heart,
but one that could still
be light with laughter.
These are the treasures that
no bank account
could ever hope to measure.

Harbor

Maybe I've
moved on from you
the way that
ships move on
from their harbors.
Free and
out to sea,
where adventures
await me,
far away from
the home
you once were
to me...

DEATH

**After the breaking,
I learned to stand on my own.
Though still—the pain gnaws.**

Now

More than anything,
it is the little things
that I miss.
The walla of
a busy cafe,
the laughter of
children on a
fresh spring day.
In this isolated
and touch-starved now,
all I can miss is
how my friends once hugged me,
how the sun once loved me,
and how peaceful
many voices in a small space
used to sound
before the whole world
went dark & silent.

After Losing You

"Did I dream it?"

The first words
I whispered
the morning after
my world ended.

I Drew Death

I drew Death
from the deck today,
and I don't know
if I really comprehend
what this card
means for me
on a day as
heavy as this.

Perhaps some
part of me must die
so that the rest of me
survives.

Maybe I'm meant
to let you go
so that who I am
can begin to flourish
and grow.

(Ten)ses

This decade
has been a minute.
Somehow I blinked
and there you were
and then I blinked
and there you weren't.
Losing you has been
a ten year yesterday
that I keep wishing
I'd wake up from.

This decade
has been an eternity.
Somehow I grew up
without you in an age
that went on and on
into a tomorrow
you would never see.
Losing you has been
a ten year forever
that I keep wishing
I could sleep through.

Thoughts from the 23

Cobblestones
and broken windows.
Churches
and worn-out soles.
Colors,
brilliant, but the paint peeling.
Catharsis
a commodity these city
corners don't get to have.

Tomorrow?

We said,
"We'll see you tomorrow..."
not knowing if
she had any left.

We crowded
around her, photos
of a life on
the wall,
a curtain
separating out
the world
she once belonged to,
while the remnants
of our family
filled the decaying air
with our joy
and our memories
and a promise of cookies
tomorrow...
the tomorrow that
never came.

On the Train to My Grandmother's Funeral

The sky at sunrise
was cardinal red,
painted with strokes of
orange,
          purple,
                    & pink.
The colors are so
alive,
and I want
you to be here
to see them.
To see the birds
soaring against
this morning's
impressionist sky.

As I watch
from the windows
of the train we
used to ride
together when
I was small enough
to sit on your lap,
I take comfort
in believing
that you're up
there in that sky,
painting these
clouds for me to see,
for me to turn into
poetry to remember
the best of you.

There's so much
I learned from you.

Tenacity.
Grace.
Faith.

You were never
perfect, but
you were a
person—
one who I loved
and who gave love
and who will be
beloved always.

Somehow, Again

My hands are still shaking,
but I manage
somehow
to pick up the pieces.
To pick up my pen
again,
somehow...

I know one day
I'll drop it
again,
when life gets hard
again.
But I know too
that my shaking hands
will keep writing words
and weaving worlds,
and that I'll be all
the stronger for
surviving

again

somehow...

My Open Letter to the Class of Whenever

My dear graduates, if only you could know what lies ahead. If I could, I would impart that you have only just begun your lives. Your black gowns adorned with colorful accomplishments and the smiles of your families are here to swaddle you into your futures, for while you don't know it yet, today, in a way, you are reborn.

Ahead of you lies forever. There are promises to be kept to make up for all the nights gone unslept in pursuit of knowledge and creativity and growth. Passing cars on Broad Street sound their horns for you, and joyful voices shout to honor your victory. Yet as triumphant as the happy scene makes me, there lingers a bitter melancholy.

Though it does not rain, the sky above us is gray, and I sit before you with my pen knowing that today, one of the students who should be among you tried to take their own life.

Their father should have been happy to watch their child finish their last semester, yet instead, he had to see that child with blood along their neck, a deep and thick cherry red.

I never found out what it was that haunted them enough to make them try to meet their end, but I tell you this so you understand that even this lowest moment was one that they survived. They made it out alive, and lived to know how loved they were, so that they could move forward and try to mend.

All I can hope is that you will keep in your hearts the knowledge that all moments, good and bad, do pass. Even when grades barely made it, there came another chance for you to try again. I hope that no matter what haunts you, you know that today, and every day, is a new beginning. A new opportunity to choose to keep living.

Ode to Peabody Hall

I stand before
empty land where
my most treasured home
one stood.
What once were halls
poured of concrete memories
and stones made of moments
are now only open air
and grass
and dirt that
looks terribly alone
without us.
The basement that
used to be filled
with energy and art
is now buried, along with
a piece of my heart.
This hallowed ground,
once filled with
sounds of joy and
heartache and
togetherness
at all hours,
now only a vacant lot
where flowers grow
in the shadow of
our misfit home,
where we sang
about finding love
in a hopeless place.

Ache of an Ember

How much must
an ember ache
in its final moments,
becoming ash?

And how free must
an ember feel
blossoming back,
a phoenix, at last?

Then

I no longer
    fear oblivion,
because I have learned
    that it doesn't exist.

I used to believe
that *this* was all there was,
but life and her lessons
have shown me there is more
beyond the expiration dates
our bodies have stamped
on all of our atoms.

    Out there and after *this*
        there is a freedom from form
            and a place where I will not
                need to change who I am
                    just to belong.

HEARTBREAK

**You didn't need me.
Turns out, I didn't need you.
I needed myself.**

Gone, But Not...

The place where we met
doesn't exist anymore,
the memories we
made there not enough
to hold the brick and mortar
together in the
face of change.

The hardest truth
to swallow is that
we don't exist
anymore either.

They say every
seven years,
your body becomes
entirely new.
Every cell of you
regenerates.
If that's true,
then there's nothing
left of me or
of you or
the place we
first began.

I hope that
means that the
next time I
see you,
we'll get to start over,
and become
something new
that won't be
forgotten.

It's Just Science

The space/time continuum
never had anything on
the power of
our chemistry,
physics bending us
toward one another
against astronomical
odds and the chemical
imbalances that
leave me feeling
so trapped in
my own mind.

I know you
to be a student of science,
but believe me when
I say there is a
magic and
artistry
connecting us
that no lab could explain.

Humans are
limited, yes,
but I must confess
that to me,
you're the one
celestial being
I'd break all
the rules for,
because my soul knows
that the two of us
are meant for more.

#Hope

Your upside-down smile
and your thumbs up
and your tears of joy
were just what
my sparkling heart
needed
to know
there might still
be #hope for us...

Starbound

I don't know if
I can do this again...
be in orbit
around someone who
doesn't look up
at the sky and
see me drifting...
I need someone
with eyes always
starbound
if ever I'm to
hear the words,
"I love you too..."

If You're Reading This...

Eyes shut
but heart open,
I imagine you're
right here and
right now and
your fingers are
tracing my lips
to where my smile
meets my eyes.

You're close enough
that soon your hands
run over my thighs,
falling in love with
every inch of me,
because everyone
before you said
there was too much
of me to ever
be beautiful.

I wish that
right here and
right now, your
mouth is only
a breath away and
that your tongue
is tasting mine,
and you're so close
that not even time
could fill the space
between us.

I know you aren't
really here,
that this is all
only a dream,

but if the day ever
comes when you are
in my arms,
maybe this poem
is one I'll let
you read.

Rooms of You

That effortless way
your laughter
wraps around me
fills me up
with as much
warmth as a
living room hearth.
It feels easy,
existing with you,
like sitting on a
wraparound porch
breathing fresh
air from the sea.
And when you
become quiet and
vulnerable,
I feel
like you're opening
a door and inviting
me in,
saying that I am worthy
of dwelling here
with you in these
rooms of you that
not everyone
is allowed to see.

Stay?

You kept the card
that I gave you close,
so it could bring you
some sun on your
rainiest days.

Why couldn't you
have kept the
rest of me close
and asked for
me to stay?

Whispered Name

Did you hear me
whispering your name
to the paper
in the middle
of the night?
Did my lovestruck verses
visit your dreams
so that when you
woke up, you were
thinking of me?
Maybe there's more
to this—to us—
than I dared imagine.
Maybe waiting for us
is a happily ever after all.

(Im)Perfect (Poetry)

this haiku is not (perfect)
but darling, neither are we
doesn't mean we're not (poetry)

Waiting For A Train

Too often
have I been
the lonely traveler,
waiting on
the empty platform
for trains
and loves
that never come.

Sometimes
a fellow traveler
runs up,
just in time
to board their
train to some other
destination where I
can't follow.

My train feels
eternally delayed,
so late that
I wonder if
it will ever
come at all.

We Were More Than Things

There was so much
meaning attached
to these arbitrary objects.

The box of matches
from that bar
we stayed
too late at.
The texts that said,
love you so much!
(even when you didn't)
The photos of us
drunk & stumbling—
smiling when we still
had reasons to.

With every
remnant of you
I get rid of,
I become more of
a stranger to myself,
struggling to relearn
who I thought I was.

I must become
someone new
outside of who
I was with you.

With every belonging
that goes into the bin
the more I begin
to realize that
it was the memories
that really made
us.

We were the
late night talks
and cover band concerts
and the cigarette breaks
I took with you,
even though
I never smoked.

We weren't any
of these physical things,
we were the
moments shared,
the things I couldn't
throw away,
even if I wanted to.

Non-Binary

The only binary thing
about us was that
we were two stars
caught up in
each other's
orbit,
where love was
our only gravity.

no ink left

i'm filling up
pages and pages
not even caring
to be bothered
with punctuation
because with you
there's no question marks
and you make me
feel like one long
run-on thought
that i never want
to end
i want you to
be the sentence
the paragraph
the friend
that i keep loving
even when there's
no ink left
in my pen

Tiny, Infinite Organs

Geodes are most
beautiful when
broken open,
shattered,
hearts laid bare.
In this state
we see all that
always was glittering
inside of them.

Maybe human hearts
are the same...
only after we've broken
can we know what
infinite glory these
tiny organs have
been holding.

DESTROY

All the words you used
against me became kindling.
I burned down the lies.

A Long Time to Grow

I'll never be
sorry enough
for all the sorrys
I shouldn't have said,
all the apologies
I made for existing.
All the times
my mind made me
believe that I
was the core
of every wrong
in the world.

I hope you know
I'm trying, even
though you think
there is only *do*
or *do not*.

Maybe doing and being
are like the creation
of the cosmos—
a big bang
that takes a
few billion years
to become.

It might not
look like I'm changing,
but beneath the
sobbing panic attacks,
plates are shifting
soil is forming
and new life
is readying to
break through

and show you
I can become
the person you
always knew I was.

You taught me
about the Spirit
and its fruits,
and while I know
you think it's taking
too long a time,
I promise
the hope in me
has roots
and I believe
soon will be
a season for
blooming.

Not This Time

Doubt is
the demon
of the day.
But it cannot
defeat me.
Not when I
have something
to say...

Punished

My healing has come from
taking every feeling
that punishes me
and leaving it
alone to starve.

Wake of Ruin

The fear that
my thoughts don't
matter to anyone
has splintered my
fingers, and for years
that fear kept
        my pen still
                my mouth shut
                        my spirit broken.

But poetry
helped me lay
r
 u
  i
   n
to the notion
that I have nothing
of value to say.

Hope ate the fear
leaving only
confidence in its
w
 a
  k
   e.

My Space

I know that
I don't always
neatly fit
into seats,
or your boxes,
or your impossible
expectations.
But I take up
the space I'm
meant to,
and whether or not
there is any of me
that might be lost
or gained,
there will never
be an inch of me
that you get to
tell me doesn't
deserve to exist.

To All the Day Jobs I Had Before

They thought by
planting me in a cage
they could
choke out my
roots, turn me
into a plastic
succulent like
the rest of them.

They didn't expect
me to fight back.

Through the bars
of my cage, I
blossomed anyway.
My weak
but unrelenting
vines spindled up
to soak in
every drop of
sun and rain
they could reach.

I've grown stronger here,
through every fear that
I wasn't tough enough
and that one day
I might just give up.

But I broke through
and my branches bloom
freely now
because no matter how
much they tried to
stifle me,
I never gave up
my will to be.

That cage lies broken
and all that remains
are the scars
of the bars
that once tried
to stop me.

At last,
I'm free to
grow deep into
the soil
and spread
seeds of hope
in those gardens
that Lin-Manuel said
I'd never get to see.

Inkblood

"Take those pens
out of your hair!"

"Don't draw
on your skin!"

Phrases my teachers
yelled at me,
not knowing my
insides are made
of ink.

They think
they can take
my stories
from my grasp,
but the last thing
I'll ever let
anyone do
is take my words
away from me.

Reclaiming My Time

Time crawls
for me now,
these days that
belong entirely to me
still in their infancy
as I relearn
how to be a
person first.

For so long
I was a servant to
someone else's watch,
beholden to that
office clock.
Expected to fake
my smiles and treat
the client like
a spoiled child
to whom everyone
must bend the knee.

Now,
my time is
mine again,
and I think
I forgot what
that freedom
felt like.
Perhaps I never
truly knew it
at all.

In my early life
I was too small to
fend for myself.

In the classroom,
I became a
statistic that
no one believed
would amount to much.
In the workforce,
surrounded by tasks
and commands,
no real encouragement
to keep learning or growing.

Now,
I'm starting over.
Humanity rebooted.
Existence reloaded.

I'm a once and future
and always queen
who belongs to
and answers to
no one but
my own heart.

Warrior Queen

My kindness
used to make me feel
like a princess who
had been locked
away in a tower
because no one
wanted to deal with
the soft-hearted,
too-sensitive
damsel in
depression.

But the more I grow,
the more I know
my kindness
makes me a warrior queen
who will not be
locked away forever.

My kindness
is fierce and loud,
and nevertheless,
persists.

So try and lock it up,
but my kindness
will never give in
so long as it lives
in a world full of
people worth
fighting for.

Mothers of Tomorrow

I think the day is coming
where we will be able to
let go of the traumas
that our own mothers
laced into our veins.

I believe we can become the
generation of mothers who
do not pick apart their children,
and who will love them in
all the ways that they exist.

REMAIN

In my darkness, I
discovered how to endure.
I exist in joy.

Seasons of Me

I'm unsure
on this uneven
late summer morning.
Can I let go of
my many ghosts,
or will they forever
cling to me
like fallen leaves
to the ground?

Autumn is coming,
and with it,
a season of dying
where summer promises
wash out to sea.
But maybe this
dying season
can be different.

Maybe those
fallen leaves can
take my hauntings
out to the gutter
so that by the time
the death and snow
of winter settles,
I'll be left only
with the seeds of me
that can bloom
back to life
in the rebirth
of spring.

Broad Street Line

Blurs of burning-out
tungsten lamps amid
shadow-soaked tunnels.

Pillars.
        Lights.
Pillars.
        Lights.
A sign of something.

Quick glimpses
of curious sun and sky
peeking through grates
that sometimes run
with rain.

This underground
passage is an
infinite mirror,
reflecting back
the darkness
of broken systems.

But look closer
at the reflections
in the thick windows
and behold
glimmers of hope
in the eyes of those
about to leave
this gathering place
and emerge into
the light of day.

No One Can See

Authenticity
is a complicated journey
to be gentler with
yourself.
It isn't always
pins or badges or pride flags...
sometimes it's staring
down the mirror
and seeing all that
is worth loving
within you.
Even when our
societies and bodies
betray us,
our hearts are
a pulsing reminder,
a thrumming truth
that no one can see
the reasons inside
that keep you existing.

Magnificent Mess

I am kind of
a mess, but that's
what makes me
magic.
When did you
ever see a spell
that was clean
and pretty?
I am the mashed-up
rose petals and the
ashes of incense.
I am the sparks
from matchboxes
and old letters getting
frayed at the edges.
I'm the glint of
moonlight on
waters dark and deep.
I'm the most
magnificent mess
that you will
ever meet.

Multitudes

Not even
the Mariana Trench
is deep enough
to contain
my multitudes.

Travel to
the moon or Mars
and still, by far,
my imagination
reaches on
and on
and on.

More sprawling
than the stars,
untameable
as the seas,
my imagination
is the glorious
most infinite
part of me.

She Doesn't Care

The sun on a beautiful day
does not care how much
you are hurting,
or that you feel broken.
She shines and smiles down
on you anyway, in hopes
that for a moment,
you might smile too.

Eclipse

When fear rises
and eclipses hope,
remember
that hope is
an ever burning light
and fear is
no more than
a passing shadow.

Don't Worry

Galaxies don't worry
that they take up
too much space,
nor are flowers bothered
by how long they
take to bloom.
So why then
do you apologize
for the time it takes
to become you?

Careful Magic

When I see birds
and blossoms of
every color, I truly
have to wonder
how anyone could
ever look upon
the cosmos
and see something
random and unplanned?

Our cells look
like universes.
Our arms share
the same veins
as flower petals,
and the light of
the sun in our eyes
is the same as the
stars in distant skies.

How could a life
filled with so much
careful magic
be nothing more
than tragic and
untempered chaos?

Be Alive

I'm learning
to be patient
with myself.
I'm remembering
to breathe
and take the time
to taste the
sweet cream in
my coffee like
it's a kind word
to my tastebuds.
I'm trying
to let go of
the pain that
adds weight to
my days that
need not be there.
I'm loving the
dazzle in my
own eyes when I
catch them in
the mirror
in the morning.
I'm smiling
because I realize
I should feel
blessed to just
be alive.

Human's Guide For Not Giving Up

First,
you must remember
what a treasure
you are.
Remember all the
microscopic ways
that the atoms
of the universe
conspired in order
to make you.

Then,
remember
how loved you are.
That someone,
somewhere in this chaotic
cosmos we call home,
loves all of you
and thinks of you
the way you do
your favorite song.

And last,
but never least,
remember that
even the most mundane
of your days is
an adventure you
have been called to.
That if you are still here,
despite every reason
you think you shouldn't be,
it is because whatever destiny
fate has in store for you
isn't finished yet.

Arrival

I think I've
been waiting for an
arrival—
a moment when
all my dreams & wantings
become tangible things
I can hold in my hands
and hug to my chest,
instead of just being
a pulsing, hoping
abstraction that
beats inside of me.

The problem, of course,
is that an
arrival
implies stopping.
Getting off the bus
because we reached
our destination.

An arrival
indicates a journey's end,
but neither we
nor our art
are finite.
With final pen strokes
begins the life of the work
that lives on long
after we've gone
back to the stardust
we were molded from.

Perhaps it's time
I remembered that an
arrival
is not what I should
be searching for.

Maybe it is
the adventure
I should enjoy living
while I still
have the chance.

* * *

Unsung Verses

selected poems

A Calling

The words summoned me,
and how could I not answer
these loves of my life?

An Invocation

A good poem
is an incantation for hope.
Use the right words
and the needed rhymes,
and you can, for a moment

— halt time —

and find a way
to believe in yourself again.

With a whispered verse
courage can stir,
or a deep thought about
the sea can spur you
to look at life
a little differently.

Every poet,
know it or not,
is an enchanter,
a magic worker using
words to conjure
faith & feeling
& forgiveness.
truth & tragedy
& tenderness.
love & longing
& loneliness.

With graphite and ink,
pixels and thought,
we invoke
that which makes
us most human—
the ability to manifest
a story from n o t h i n g.

The Road So Far

I feel like I fell asleep
in the passenger seat,
and woke up a thousand miles
from where I last remember.

I wonder how I got this far
when the depressed slumber kept me
numb.
How many sights and trees did I miss
passing by when my eyes were closed,
and I, lost to unconsciousness?

So I look to the driver's side,
surprised, because the one
behind the wheel is me.

"I don't understand..."
I say to my driving-self,
but they just smile.

"It's okay, you've been through much
and needed the rest more than me.
I'm happy to get us where we
need to be."

"So who are you?" I ask them,
wondering how along all these
rocky roads and through the dark night,
they managed to keep driving
without ever getting tired.

"Your Hope, so don't worry.
We're almost there."

"Almost where?"

And with a confidence I fully believe,
they just wink at me.

So I lean my head back on the window,
doing my best to stay
awake for the ride,
but trusting that if I need
to sleep, my Hope will
always drive me.

Through These Doors

Though I have never held their key,
these doors hold behind them
an entire world to me.

From the moment I saw them,
I sensed their magic,
something ancient lurking
just on the other side
of the dense blue metal.

These doors made me realize
that we always have the power
to make portals of the ordinary.

Lewis gave me a wardrobe.
MacHale gave me an abandoned subway.
L'Engle gave me love & spacetime itself.
So why not a simple set of doors
beneath a bridge over
the Delaware's water?

Why not me,
a nobody to the cosmos,
yet the writer of
my own story?

An Author's Last Words

The time draws near
where you won't belong
to me anymore,
because you will belong
to the world.

While part of my
heart aches knowing
you will go on to
live beyond me,
I try to remember
that this isn't a letting go —
it is a loving surrender.

The Adventure Begins (Again)

I wrote you onto
the back of the book
so that I never
forget where I began.

As the sun sinks
russet pink on Market,
I'm reminded of
a tiny room
with no physical windows,
but where between equations,
I dreamed a creation —
a world across the stars
where characters with magic
might discover who they are.

I wonder often
what I'd say to
my younger self
if I could speak to
them, knowing
what I know now...
but the truth is
that I'd just smile
from a distance
and rest in the knowing
that every mistake
they are destined to make
will lead them to this life
that's more glorious and grand
than they could ever imagine.

If the Moon Only Knew

Do you think the moon knows
how loved they are?
That on a rock somewhere
they will never touch,
entire worlds worth
of people will pen
painful, yearning, honest
verses about them?

Do they know that
one human's footprint
on their surface is but
a symbol for the billions
across time that have
sang songs of their beauty
and strung together
similes about their light
and wrote entire mythologies
of their love affair
with the sun and stars?

Did they know how
Sappho and Shakespeare
would immortalize line
after line about them
with longing, or that
somewhere in the
twenty-first century,
some broke poet from Philly
would find such sweet comfort
in the sight of them that

said poet would weave them
irrevocably into the fabric
of their most beloved story?

Maybe the moon will
never know how loved they are.
But I'd rather spend my nights
hoping we exist in
a universe where they do.

An Old Friend

Every winter I wait
patiently for my
old friend Orion
to return to the
crystal clear heavens,
for he has always
served as a reminder
of another year I survived.
There is nowhere I feel
more at home and alive
than beneath the infinity
of Orion's guarded sky.

Reverence

There are cultures of
the world that wear
white for their funerals.

Perhaps that is why
it snows in winter,
and why the silence of
winter's first falling holds
all the reverence
of a wake.

Nature is in mourning,
every tear a snowflake.

An Ode to Norwood Christmas Eves

All the cheer is boxed up,
tucked away in the dusty corner
of an attic with a broken ladder.

I can't climb back into those
long-gone holidays anymore.

I'm starting to forget
the smell of laughter
and the sound of sugar cookies.
All these sensory memories
of Christmases past
swirl together, feeling about as real
as the Kinkade yuletide painting
that used to hang in the hallway.

I wonder what those
holy nights look like
in the divergent timeline
where you didn't die...

Is the house still ours?

Do we have the wood burning stove
going, making the whole place
fresh with the aroma of
deep winter incense?

Is our fake tree still covered in
50 years of glitter and
glass-blown family memories?

Are Dolly and Kenny
blaring from the CD player,
declaring how it just isn't
Christmas without you?

Is the living room filled
with our dearest friends,
all stopping by for a plate
and a piece of home?

The Gift of Fire

Two years ago was the last day of the old world.
We are still trying to find our way back,
but I think the flaw in that plan is
that there is no way back,
there is only forward.

We are forging a new world now,
one where we've realized that maybe
strangers are not as kind as we'd hoped,
where we're teetering on the
fine line of a tightrope,
praying with all we have left
that we won't plunge into the
abyss that lurks below.

But even in this age of shadow,
there are soft promises of light
shining out in the little things,
neighbors helping neighbors,
friends reminding us to breathe,
family that we can hold again,
even if at a bit of a distance.

When Prometheus gave us fire,
the true gift was how we gathered,
realizing there's nothing that matters
more than loving one another
and telling tales over broken bread.

We must remember that
true fires are more than a place
where we come together —

those tiny, flickering flames
also glow within us,
keeping us warm in this,
our generation's longest night.

A New Year's Eve Reflection

Rest
now,
knowing
this ending
did not destroy you.
You are always just beginning.

a new year's day intention

maybe living in
my own skin
can be beautiful.

maybe even if
i can't manage
to sing entire songs
of self love,
i can manage
a verse or two
of self kindness.

maybe this doesn't
need to be
the best year ever
to be a year
that holds
small good things.

Late winter love story

saw the first burst
of gold from the ground
just as the sun decided
to step out from
behind the clouds.

how i wish humans
were as joyful
in their meetings,
the way the sun sends
her loving greetings,
light kissing the cheeks
of every leaf and petal,
because she unapologetically
loves them all the same.

presence

before i could
even open the notebook,
they were gone...

their laughter leaves
with a brush of breeze,
and i know for sure
i'll never see them again.

but somewhere down the road,
that little girl that i watched
waddle into her mother's arms
will look back at
the photos her dad snapped
and i'll be there
just out of frame—
someone she'll never know,
an energy in the background,
as visible as the wind
that whisked them away.

the fall

i thought i had
shattered my teeth,
splintered the bones
in my face, my eyes
awash with white hot tears
and my hand
covered in blood
when i touched my mouth.

as i sobbed at my reflection,
all i thought was,
"this is what you get
for daring to hope"

yet in all that mess,
nothing was broken.
everything felt ruined,
when in reality,
everything was fine.

that night would go on
to be a joyful memory
of cheap wine
and yearning verses
and breaking curses,
but i have to wonder
if all that would have
been as sweet
had i not first
survived the fall?

you were

~~you walked away when~~
~~i finally became myself~~
~~and i don't know if~~
~~that's something i'll~~
~~ever recover from.~~
~~this was the beginning~~
~~of all i ever dreamed~~
~~and you were~~
~~supposed to be here.~~
~~you weren't~~
~~supposed to be~~
~~crossed out lines~~
~~in my story.~~
~~i hope more than anything~~
~~that one day you'll write~~
yourself back into the narrative...

aren't we all

(After Sue Williamson & Lebohang Kganye's 'Tell Me What You Remember')

all over these walls
are stories of the long gone
and the somehow enduring,
people from a country
on the other side of the world
who will never know my name
or that i've witnessed them
and tried to imagine their lives.

what does that make their legacy?
or mine?
how do we quantify storytelling
through time?

these lives all become
legends one day,
ancient tales
& half remembered truths
of the hopes we had
when we were still here...

but aren't we all,
every one of us,
the dead and the living,
the thriving and the dying,
all, always, were & will be

here?

from someone who survived it

a line for each of you
a verse for the forgotten
you fought so hard to be here
and the sun will rise again, dear
just keep your eyes skyward,
and know you'll make it out of here

season's CHILD

i was born as summer died
but i've always belonged to autumn—
crisp nights under clear skies
that smell of leaves reuniting
with the soil they grew from,
all of nature painting itself warm
even as the nights bend colder.
the famous rhyme reads,
thursday's child has far to go,
but i just want to stop and know

how much further?

how many more seasons
must i endure before i know
the peace that faith promises?
how many more dissociated rotations
around a sun i'll never touch
must i go through before
i may lay my weary head to rest?

finding out

melancholy notes
and ironic jokes.
sexy explorations
of the spiritual,
and soul searching
questions begged
with searing, millennial wit.

there's nothing in
this world like this—
strangers together,
captivated by
the profoundly human
experience of
making things
and fucking up
and finding out
that the thing still
ended up beautiful.

the singer sang,
"we have nothing in common"
and the poet posited
that "you can't fail",
but i'd argue
that our magic & our glory
lies in the one thing
we all have in common...
we're all failing everyday,
but we're still here,
existing anyway.

this is our legacy

the past will paint
you a portrait of
"poetry isn't"
they've only developed
the negative narrative
of what they believed
poetry *shouldn't* be

either it shouldn't be free verse,
or it doesn't rhyme enough,
it shouldn't be so formal or
shouldn't say words like fuck

but what we
are endeavoring to be
is the generation of
"poetry is"
we are the moment reveling
in all poetry *can* be

poetry is soft and poetry is slutty
poetry is asexual and poetry is non-binary
poetry is loud war cries and quiet why nots
poetry is our memories and the ones we forgot
poetry is how we hurt and how we heal
poetry is speculative dreams
and the truths we reveal

poetry is love, poetry is loss
poetry is aching, poetry is art

we are the identities
society would rather
stay silent and compliant,
but instead we rejoice
and we rebel, soaking in
the love letters of our ancestors
and wringing out new verses
for the children that follow us

what we are building
in back rooms of bars
and Kensington living rooms
and in manic, midnight group chats
is how history will remember us,
maybe not by name
but by these movements
we've made and
the lives we've changed,
because just as the drop
never sees how far
their ripples reach,
so too will we
never meet all the ones
our words will touch...
but we can take heart
in knowing that
our legacy of
poetry is
enough

the poem at the end of this book

i come back to you now,
my first verse child
and my second chapter,
with this glance to the future,
realizing deeply
that i am not the same
soul who began you.

fear prevailed then,
a younger mind convinced
all that mattered
were the numbers,
not the meanings.
how many reached?
how many copies?
how many dollars?
i lost myself
in all those integers,
as if numerics
were the only way
to measure my success.

i did not celebrate you
as i should have,
something i fear
every creator must
suffer at least once,
but as i come back to you now,
i hope you know
i wouldn't be here without you.

my second chapter
came to life
as the old world was dying,
making way for
the epoch of social distance,
an age where
cloth masks went on
& dissociative masks
were ripped off.
you were a phoenix
from the ashes
of the smoldering before,
and for that, my child,
you'll always be
my noblest warrior.

i let you both rest a while,
while i took a journey
across the stars
to tell the first tale
of your sister world,
of a girl named Piper
who was at last ready
for her adventure
to begin.

i come back to you now,
a little wiser & entire
worlds kinder to myself.
your words, while they may
not have reached far,

have fortified my heart
into one that believes
themselves worthy
of beating.

i think how in a film
from my childhood,
Gene Wilder said,
"you must go forwards
to go back..."
and that,
my book i am about
to open is who you are.

you are me
moving on through
an edition that honors
where and who
i've come from.
you are the verses
that made me,
you are the art
that saved me.
my past,
my future,
& my moment—
let these words
that i've lived
not be my last.

* * *

Acknowledgements

When it came time to write the acknowledgements for UNRAVELING LIGHT and DARKNESS UNDONE, my mission was simple. Do my best to thank every person I could think of who had in ways both large and small, impacted me and led to the publication of my first poetic works.

As I sit here now, trying to think of who it is I should be thanking for this combined edition however, I've decided to take a slightly different approach and use this space to thank the one person who I never thank enough—myself.

I don't say this to sound egotistical, but rather because I've spent more of my life than not being severely unkind to myself, believing all the terrible things that bullies said about me. I spent my first two decades internalizing the hatred that society at large had for bodies and identities like mine. Then the journey of the last ten years for me—falling in love with poetry, finding my voice, learning how to care for myself even on the days when the depression or anxiety or sheer loneliness were kicking my ass—has been all at once the hardest and most beautiful thing I've ever had to go through. I conquered demons that used to make me cower in fear. I found family and community in the most unlikely of places. I don't win every single day, but for the first time in my life, there are more bright days than dark. When things start to feel overwhelming, I have more joy to dwell on that helps outweigh the sadness. I never thought this would happen, and so to be here celebrating that growth with a new edition of the first stories that helped me become that person, thanking myself for surviving feels fitting.

And with this dear reader, I also want to thank you, and hope you'll take this moment to stop, reflect, and thank yourself too. YOU are the reason you are still here, despite all the places, people, and things that may have tried to make sure you weren't.

You're here, reading these words and finding hope where you can.
Taking life one sentence at a time, unfolding your own beautiful story,
that I hope you too will get the chance to share with the world someday.
I'm endlessly grateful for you, and hope you are for yourself too.

About the Author

Elayna Mae Darcy is a queer poet, YA author, filmmaker and star cluster of feels. With a passion for engaging in fandom communities, they have written articles, spoken on panels at both New York and San Diego Comic Cons, and co-host/produce the fandom podcasts—*Saving People, Queering Things* and *Fine Things Well*.

They have had short stories and poems published in *Wizards in Space Literary Magazine*, *tiny wren lit*, and *just femme & dandy*, and are the author of the UNVEIL ME poetry duology, and the YA novel in verse, STILL THE STARS, which is the first book of the Oreanam Trilogy. Originally from Norristown, PA, they currently live in North Philadelphia with one of their dearest friends, and a very snuggly cat named Bean.

elaynamusings.com

twitter | @elaynamae
instagram | @elaynamusings
tiktok | @destielayna

sign up for their newsletter

Queery Letters

at elayna.substack.com

Made in the USA
Columbia, SC
04 April 2023

f5b093e0-4009-4ab6-baf2-a641224002ffR01